John Bro

OHN BROWN's RAID

National Park Service History Series

Office of Publications, National Park Service,
U.S. Department of the Interior, Washington, D.C.

1973

The text of this booklet was prepared by the staff of the Office of Publications and is based on National Park Service reports by William C. Everhart and Arthur L. Sullivan.

National Park Handbooks are published to support the National Park Service's management programs and to promote understanding and enjoyment of the more than 350 National Park System sites, which represent important examples of our country's natural and cultural inheritance. Each handbook is intended to be informative reading and a useful guide before, during, and after a park visit. More than 100 titles are in print. They are sold at parks and can be purchased by mail from the Superintendent of Documents, U.S. Government Printing Office, Washington, DC 20402.

Harpers Ferry National Historical Park is administered by the National Park Service, U.S. Department of the Interior. A superintendent, whose address is Harpers Ferry, WV 25425, is in immediate charge.

Library of Congress Cataloging in Publication Data

United States National Park Service.
John Brown's raid.
National Park Service history series
Supt. of Docs. no.: 129-2: J61/4.
1. Harpers Ferry, W. Va.-John Brown Raid, 1859. I. Title II. Series: United States. National Park Service. History series.
E451.U58   1974   973.7'116   73-600184

*"All through the conflict, up and down
Marched Uncle Tom and Old John Brown,
One ghost, one form ideal;
And which was false and which was true,
And which was mightier of the two,
The wisest sibyl never knew.
For both alike were real."*

*Oliver Wendell Holmes
June 14, 1882*

This view of Harpers Ferry from Maryland Heights in 1859 appeared in Frank Leslie's Illustrated Newspaper shortly after John Brown's raid brought the town to national prominence.

⟨ JOHN BROWN's RAID

Through the gloom of the night, Sunday, October 16, 1859, a small band of men tramped silently behind a horse-drawn wagon down a winding Maryland road leading to Harpers Ferry, Va. From the shoulder of each man hung loosely a Sharps rifle, hidden by long gray shawls that protected the ghostly figures against the chilling air of approaching winter. A slight drizzle of rain veiled the towering Blue Ridge Mountains with an eerie mist. Not a sound broke the stillness, save the tramping feet and the creaking wagon.

Side by side marched lawyer and farmer, escaped convict and pious Quaker, spiritualist and ex-slave, joined in common cause by a hatred of slavery. Some had received their baptism of fire in "Bleeding Kansas," where a bitter 5-year war between pro-slavery and anti-slavery factions left death and destruction in its wake and foreshadowed a larger conflict to come. Most were students of guerrilla tactics; all were willing to die to free the slaves.

This strange little force, five Negroes and 14 whites, was the "Provisional Army of the United States," about to launch a fantastic scheme to rid the country of its "peculiar institution" once and for all, a scheme conjured up by the fierce-eyed, bearded man seated on the wagon—"Commander in Chief" John Brown. He was the planner, the organizer, the driving force, the reason why these men were trudging down this rough Maryland road to an uncertain fate.

THE ROAD TO HARPERS FERRY

This man who would electrify the Nation and bring it closer to civil war by his audacious attack on slavery was born at Torrington, Conn., on May 9, 1800, the son of Owen and Ruth Mills Brown. The Browns were a simple, frugal, and hard-working family. They had a deep and abiding interest in religion, and from earliest childhood John Brown was taught the value of strong religious habits. He was required, along with his brothers and sisters, to participate in daily Bible reading and prayer sessions. "Fear God & keep his commandments" was his father's constant admonition. It was also his father who taught him to view the enslavement of Negroes as a sin against God.

In 1805 the Browns, like many other families of the period, moved west to Ohio. There, in the little settlement of Hudson, about 25 miles south of Cleveland, John grew to manhood. He received little formal education; most of what he learned came from what he afterwards called the "School of adversity." He cared little for studies, preferring life in the open. Consistently choosing the "hardest & roughest" kinds of play because they afforded him "almost the only compensation for the confinement & restraints of school," he was extremely proud of his

The future abolitionist and martyr in the cause of Negro freedom was born in this stark, shutterless farmhouse in Torrington, Conn. He lived here only 5 years. In 1805 his father, Owen Brown (above), sold the farm and moved the family west to Ohio.

ability to "wrestle, & Snow ball, & run, & jump, & knock off old seedy Wool hats."

When John was 8 years old his mother died, and for awhile he believed that he would never recover from so "complete & permanent" a loss. His father remarried, but John never accepted his stepmother emotionally and "continued to pine after his own Mother for years."

An indifferent student, and "not . . . much of a schollar" anyway, John quit school and went to work at his father's tannery. Owen Brown, who had been a tanner and a shoemaker before moving to Hudson, had already taught his son the art of dressing leather from "Squirel, Raccoon, Cat, Wolf, or Dog Skins," and John soon displayed remarkable ability in the trade. When the War of 1812 broke out, Owen contracted to supply beef to the American forces in Michigan. He gave John the task of rounding up wild steers and other cattle in the woods and then driving them, all by himself, to army posts more than 100 miles away. Contact with the soldiers and their profanity and lack of discipline so disgusted young Brown that he later resolved to pay fines rather than take part in the militia drills required of all Hudson males of a certain age.

It was during the war, or so Brown later claimed, that he first came to understand what his father meant about the evil of slavery. He had just completed one of his cattle drives and was staying with a "very gentlemanly landlord" who owned a slave about the same age as John. The Negro boy was "badly clothed, poorly fed . . . & beaten before his eyes with Iron Shovels or any other thing that came first to hand."

John Brown had not yet grown his famous beard when this picture was taken in Kansas in 1856. Though 3 years away from the deed that would make his name immortal, he had already begun his private war against slavery.

Mary Ann Day, Brown's loyal and self-sacrificing second wife, stoically endured her husband's constant wanderings in business and anti-slavery activities. She is shown here about 1851 with two of their daughters, Annie and Sarah.

Outraged by this, John returned home "a most determined Abolitionist" swearing "Eternal war with Slavery."

In 1816 John joined the Congregational Church in Hudson and soon developed a strong interest in becoming a minister. For a while he attended a divinity school in Plainfield, Mass., then transferred to another school in Litchfield, Conn. At that time Litchfield was a center of abolitionist sentiment; it was also the birthplace of Harriet Beecher Stowe, whose book Uncle Tom's Cabin, published in 1852, would stir passions North and South, win international support for the anti-slavery cause, and help to bring on civil war in 1861. How much of Litchfield's abolitionist atmosphere young Brown absorbed is not known. A shortage of funds and an inflammation of the eyes forced him to return to Ohio in the summer of 1817. His dream of becoming a minister was forever shattered, but he never lost his religious fervor.

When he was 20 years old, "led by his own inclination & prompted also by his Father," Brown married Dianthe Lusk, a "remarkably plain" and pious girl a year younger than himself. She died 12 years later, in August 1832, following the birth of their seventh child. Brown remarried within a year, and fathered 13 children by his second wife, Mary Ann Day. In a never-ending struggle to feed and clothe his growing family, Brown drifted through Ohio, Pennsylvania, New York, Connecticut, and Massachusetts plying many trades. He worked at tanning, surveying, and farming; at times he was shepherd, cattleman, wool merchant, and postmaster; for a while he bred race horses and speculated in real estate. Uniformly unsuccessful in these ventures, Brown's debts mounted, and he was barely able to keep his large family from starvation.

Despite his frequent business reversals and his strenuous and consuming efforts to support his family, Brown never abandoned his intense desire to free enslaved Negroes from bondage. His first opportunity to strike a blow at the institution he hated so much came in Kansas, where, following the passage of the Kansas-Nebraska Act in 1854, pro-slavery "Border Ruffians" clashed brutally with anti-slavery "Jayhawkers" over the extension of slavery to Kansas and Nebraska Territories.

Five of Brown's sons—Owen, Jason, Frederick, Salmon, and John, Jr.—had emigrated to Kansas and joined the free-soil cause. When they appealed to their father for help in May 1855, Brown, another son Oliver, and son-in-law Henry Thompson rushed to Kansas and plunged into the conflict with a fury. As captain of the "Liberty Guards," a quasi-militia company that he himself formed, Brown shortly gained national notoriety as a bold and ruthless leader.

For the next several years, murders, bushwhackings, lynchings, and burnings were common occurrences, and the territory was aptly named "Bleeding Kansas." Atrocity matched atrocity. When pro-slavery forces sacked and burned the town of Lawrence in May 1856, Brown was outraged.

John Brown, Jr., the oldest of Brown's sons, fought alongside his father in Kansas. The Pottawatomie murders, in which he took no part, caused him to suffer a mental collapse from which he never fully recovered. Nevertheless, in 1859 he was entrusted with forwarding the weapons for the attack on Harpers Ferry from Ohio to Chambersburg, Pa.

Proclaiming himself an instrument of God's will, he, with four of his sons and three others, deliberately and brutally murdered five pro-slavery men along the banks of Pottawatomie Creek. In the months that followed, Brown terrorized the Missouri-Kansas border by a series of bloody guerrilla attacks that brought him to the attention of the Nation's abolitionist faction. In late August 1856, about a month before he left Kansas, Brown and his men clashed with pro-slavery Missourians at the small settlement of Osawatomie. That action earned him the nickname "Osawatomie" and cost him the life of his son Frederick. It also hardened his stand against slavery. "I have only a short time to live—only one death to die," he said, "and I will die fighting for this cause. There will be no more peace in this land until slavery is done for. I will give them something else to do than to extend slave territory. I will carry this war into Africa."

The attack on Harpers Ferry was the culmination of a plan Brown had evolved many years before he went to Kansas. By the early 1850's he had come to believe that a location within the slave States should be selected where raids on slave plantations could be easily carried out and the freed bondsmen sent to safety in the North. Convinced that mountains throughout history had enabled the few to defend themselves against the many, he believed that even against regular Army troops a small force operating from a mountain stronghold could hold out indefinitely and provide sanctuary for freed slaves, who would be supplied with arms to

Three of John Brown's most trusted lieutenants in the Harpers Ferry raid were (clockwise) John E. Cook, Aaron D. Stevens, and John H. Kagi.

fight for their liberty. Brown had decided, from studying European fortifications and military operations, that somewhere along the Allegheny Mountain chain a small force could achieve those objectives.

In the autumn of 1857, on his second trip to Kansas, Brown began recruiting his force for the projected raid. Among the first to join him were three young veterans of the Kansas fighting: John E. Cook, Aaron D. Stevens, and John H. Kagi. Each would play an important role in the attack on Harpers Ferry.

Cook, 27-year-old member of a wealthy Connecticut family, had attended Yale University and studied law in New York City before going to Kansas in 1855. He stood about 5 feet 5 inches tall, had long, silk-blond hair that curled about his neck, and "his deep blue eyes were gentle in expression as a woman's." Brown's son Salmon, who knew Cook in Ohio and Kansas, characterized him as "highly erratic" in temperament "and not overly stocked with morality. He was the best pistol-shot I ever saw. . . . [and] just as much of an expert in getting into the good graces of the girls." He loved to "talk and rattle on about himself."

Stevens, then 26 years old, was, like Cook, a native of Connecticut. He ran away from home at the age of 16 and joined the Massachusetts Volunteer Regiment to fight in the Mexican War. Honorably discharged at the end of that conflict, he found civilian life so boring that he enlisted as a bugler in a United States dragoon regiment in the West and took part in several campaigns against the Navaho and Apache Indians. Stevens possessed an explosive temper, and at Taos, N. Mex., in the mid-1850's, he nearly killed an officer in a drunken brawl and was sentenced to death. President Franklin Pierce commuted the sentence to 3 years' hard labor at Fort Leavenworth, Kansas. In January 1856 Stevens escaped and joined the Free-State cause. As colonel of the Second Kansas Volunteer Regiment, he fought in some of the territory's bloodiest battles. Standing just over 6 feet tall, Stevens was a powerfully built man who could wield a saber with deadly skill. He had black curly hair, "black, brooding eyes," and a full beard. In his youth he had been a choir boy (his father and elder brothers taught singing), had a rich baritone voice, and liked to sing. Totally dedicated to the overthrow of slavery, he once told a Kansas sheriff: "We are in the right, and will resist the universe."

Kagi, an Ohio lad of 22, was largely self-educated and had taught school in Virginia until his abolitionist views got him into trouble with local officials and he had to flee the State. Traveling to Kansas in 1856, he became a lawyer in Nebraska City. Occasionally he served as a court stenographer or shorthand reporter. He also functioned as a correspondent for several Eastern newspapers and John Brown dubbed him "our Horace Greeley." While riding with Stevens' Second Kansas Regiment in 1856, Kagi was taken prisoner by Federal troops and served 4 months in jail before being released on bail. In January 1857 he was shot by a pro-slavery judge during a disagreement and was still suffering from his wounds when he joined Brown. Tall, with angular features, Kagi was usually unkempt, unshaven, and generally unimpressive in appearance;

Brown's target was the United States Armory and Arsenal at Harpers Ferry, shown here in an 1857 lithograph.

but he was articulate and highly intelligent, of serene temperament, and not easily aroused. "His fertility of resources made him a tower of strength to John Brown," wrote George B. Gill, an Iowa youth who signed up for the raid but defected before it took place. "He was a logician of more than ordinary ability. He was full of wonderful vitality and all things were fit food for his brain."

When he enlisted them, Brown told Cook, Stevens, and Kagi only that he was organizing a company of men to resist pro-slavery aggressions. He did not tell them where he planned to take them. When seven more volunteers joined the group at Tabor, Iowa, he informed his recruits that their "ultimate destination was the State of Virginia." Shortly afterwards the men finally learned that Harpers Ferry was the probable target. Kagi, who had once taught school in the area, gave Brown valuable information about the town. The place fitted Brown's requirements perfectly. It lay near the mountains he counted upon to afford a hiding place, and it was on the border of Virginia, a slave State, only 40 miles from the free State of Pennsylvania. It also contained an United States armory and arsenal, where much-needed arms were stored.

After a trip to New England to raise funds, Brown called a "Constitutional Convention" of his followers to meet on May 8, 1858, at Chatham, Ontario, Canada. Besides Brown's group, 34 Negroes attended the meeting and heard the Kansas guerrilla chieftain outline his plan for the deliverance of their enslaved brethren. First, he told them, he intended to strike at a point in the South. This blow would be followed by a general slave uprising in which even free Negroes in the Northern States and Canada would flock to his banner. He would lead them into the mountains and "if any hostile action . . . were taken against us, either by the militia of the separate States or by the armies of the United States, we purposed to defeat first the militia, and next, if it were possible, the troops of the United States . . . ."

The convention unanimously adopted a "Provisional Constitution and Ordinances for the People of the United States" to serve as the law of the land while the army of liberation instituted a new government—one that would not supplant but exist side-by-side with the U.S. Government and which would explicitly prohibit slavery. John Brown was elected "Commander in Chief" of the new provisional army to be formed, other officers were appointed, and the convention adjourned. Before leaving again for New England to gather supplies and money for the attack, Brown sent Cook to Harpers Ferry to act as a spy; the others scattered, seeking employment to maintain themselves until called together for the march into Virginia.

To equip, maintain, and transport the men needed to carry out his plan, Brown required a considerable amount of money and weapons. He had neither, but because of his Kansas activities, he was able to enlist the support of Northern abolitionists in his fight against slavery.

Samuel Gridley Howe   Thomas Wentworth Higginson

Franklin B. Sanborn

George Luther Stearns

Gerrit Smith

Theodore Parker

The moral and financial
backing of these men, known
as "The Secret Six," made
the raid on Harpers Ferry
possible.

Philosophers, scholars, religious leaders, philanthropists, and businessmen gave freely but discretely to the cause. Chief among Brown's backers was a secret committee of six: Dr. Samuel Gridley Howe, Boston, Mass., educator, minister, and reformer; Thomas Wentworth Higginson, militant clergyman of Worcester, Mass.; Theodore Parker, Boston's outstanding Unitarian minister; Franklin B. Sanborn, editor and schoolmaster of Concord, Mass.; Gerrit Smith, former New York Congressman and a great Peterboro, N.Y., landowner; and George L. Stearns, industrialist and merchant of Medford, Mass. Through them Brown received most of the money and weapons that enabled him to launch his attack.

RENDEZVOUS FOR REVOLUTION

By the summer of 1859 Harpers Ferry was a quietly thriving little industrial and transportation community sitting on a narrow shelf of land at the confluence of the Potomac and Shenandoah Rivers in the Blue Ridge Mountains of northern Virginia. Until its selection as the site for a Federal armory at the end of the 18th century, the town's growth had been slow. What growth it did experience was due to its location on the wilderness route to the Shenandoah Valley. The land on which the town sat was first settled in 1733 by a Pennsylvania Dutchman named Peter Stephens, who operated a small ferryboat service across the rivers. At that time the place was called "Peter's Hole" because it was dominated by three towering bluffs—Maryland Heights to the north, Loudoun Heights to the south, and Bolivar Heights to the west. When Robert Harper, a skilled Philadelphia architect and millwright, bought the land in 1747, he improved the ferry service and built a gristmill. Around these facilities at the base of Bolivar Heights the village of Harpers Ferry gradually developed.

In 1794, when relations between the United States and England were strained, Congress grew uneasy over the country's military posture. Uncertain of the ordnance-producing capabilities of private manufacturers in time of need, it directed President George Washington to establish a number of armories where guns could be made and stored. One of the sites he chose was Harpers Ferry.

Washington was well acquainted with Harpers Ferry. As a young man during the middle part of the century, he had accompanied surveying parties that inspected the vast holdings of the Virginia aristocracy in this area. He considered Harpers Ferry "the most eligible spot on the [Potomac] river" for an armory. Abundant water power was available, iron ore was plentiful nearby, hardwood forests insured a steady supply of charcoal to fuel the forges, and the place was far enough inland to be secure from foreign invasion.

In June 1796 the Government purchased from the Harper heirs a 125-acre tract of land and began constructing workshops on the benchland between the Potomac River and what would later become Potomac Street. Waterpower was harnessed by building a dam upstream from the armory and channeling the water through a canal into the workshops. Although a critical shortage of gunsmiths and ordnance-making machinery restricted operations for several years, limited arms production began late in 1798 under the direction of an English Moravian named Joseph Perkin, the armory's first superintendent.

The first muskets, based on the old French infantry type of 1763, were completed in 1801. In 1803 production was expanded to include rifles, and 2 years later the manufacture of pistols. (The Model 1805 pistol, made at Harpers Ferry, was the first hand weapon to be produced at a United States armory.) At first the rate of musket production was meager, but by 1810 the armory was turning out 10,000 annually, storing them in two arsenal buildings nearby on Shenandoah Street.

In 1819 John Hall, a Maine gunsmith, received a contract from the Federal Government to manufacture 1,000 breech-loading flintlock rifles of his own design. Sent to Harpers Ferry, he set up the Hall Rifle Works in two buildings on Lower Hall Island, which adjoined Virginius Island in the Shenandoah River about ½ mile from its junction with the Potomac. Hall's rifles were made on so exact a scale that all the parts were interchangeable—a factor that helped to pave the way for modern mass production methods. The War Department was elated with Hall's success and his contract was repeatedly renewed. When the Hall rifle was discontinued in 1844, the Government tore down the old buildings and erected a new rifle factory on the same site. Standard U.S. Model rifles were produced there until the industry was destroyed, along with the armory complex, at the outbreak of the Civil War in 1861.

The abundance of water power that had attracted the arms industry soon brought others. Besides the rifle factories on Hall Island, Virginius Island boasted an iron foundry, flour mill, cotton mill, and machine shop, all powered by water diverted through the island by a dam in the Shenandoah River and a series of sluiceways and underground water tunnels. More than 200 persons made their home around the prospering island industries.

The formation, development, and expansion of the United States Armory and Arsenal at Harpers Ferry (its complete, official designation) was the chief stimulus for the growth of the town. From a simple beginning the armory by 1859 had spread to include 20 workshops and offices, lined in a neat double row over an area 600 yards long. At its peak, the armory provided employment for more than 400 men, mostly transplanted Northerners whom local residents classified as "foreigners." In the 65-year history of this major industry, the U.S. Government invested nearly $2 million in land, water power improvements, walls and embankments, hydraulic machinery, and buildings.

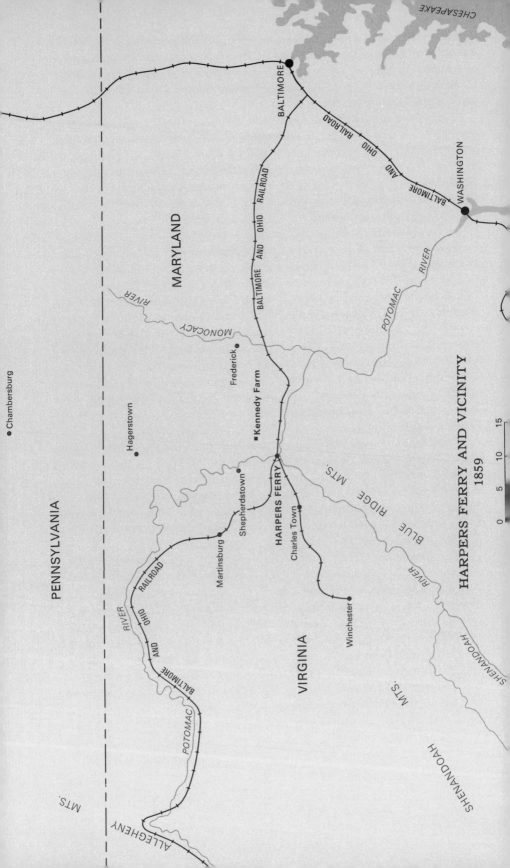

CHESAPEAKE

PENNSYLVANIA

● Chambersburg

ALLEGHENY MTS.

MARYLAND

MONOCACY RIVER

Hagerstown

Frederick

■ Kennedy Farm

Shepherdstown

Martinsburg

BALTIMORE AND OHIO RAILROAD

POTOMAC RIVER

HARPERS FERRY

Charles Town

Winchester

VIRGINIA

BLUE RIDGE MTS.

SHENANDOAH RIVER

SHENANDOAH MTS.

BALTIMORE

BALTIMORE AND OHIO RAILROAD

WASHINGTON

POTOMAC RIVER

HARPERS FERRY AND VICINITY
1859

0   5   10   15

After 1830 Harpers Ferry, already recognized as an important industrial center, attained prominence as a vital link in the transportation and communications line between the Ohio and Shenandoah Valleys and the East. By 1830 a semi-weekly stagecoach service connected the town with Washington, D.C. The one-way trip usually required a full day's travel. That same year a turnpike company was founded to construct a 16-mile macademized toll road from Harpers Ferry to Middleway, 5 miles west of Charles Town. A turnpike being built from Frederick, Md., about 20 miles to the east, reached the town in 1832. Still another turnpike company, organized in 1851, ran a road from Harpers Ferry southeastward to Hillsborough, about 10 miles away.

But the signal impetus to the establishment of the town's commercial position was the arrival of canal and railroad. Waging a bitter battle to reach the rich Ohio Valley and carry its trade to the East, impeding each other's progress at every opportunity, the Chesapeake and Ohio Canal (originating in Washington, D.C.) and the Baltimore and Ohio Railroad (originating in Baltimore, Md.) reached Harpers Ferry in the early 1830's. Following the winding Potomac River northward and westward from Georgetown, the C & O Canal arrived at Harpers Ferry in November 1833, more than a year ahead of its rival. But the railroad pushed on to the Ohio Valley while the canal stopped at Cumberland, Md. The establishment of these two arteries provided shippers with a cheaper carrier for their products and assured travelers of a more efficient and economical means of reaching their destinations.

With the expansion of industry and the development of superior transportation facilities, the population of the community swelled to nearly 3,000 by 1859. Of these about 150 were "free coloreds" and 150 were slaves. The total number of slaves in the entire six-county area around Harpers Ferry was just slightly more than 18,000, of which less than 5,000 were men. There were no large plantations because the land and the climate could not sustain a plantation economy. The few slaveholders maintained farms, and their blacks were mainly "well-kept house-servants."

Most of the white residents of Harpers Ferry worked at the armory or at the manufacturing plants on Virginius Island. Because land was at a premium, the houses, saloons, hotels, and shops were tightly aligned along Shenandoah, Potomac, and High Streets, and sprawled up the slopes of Bolivar Heights. In some places the rocky cliffs were blasted away to make room for another building. Most of the homes were of simple design, but the Government-built residences of the armory officials were more elaborate.

The inhabitants of the town were chiefly of Irish, English, and German descent. Besides building six churches of varying faiths (one of which, St. Peter's Catholic Church, is still standing and in use today), they established five private girls' schools. A man could get a drink at the Gault House or take a meal at the Potomac Restaurant or the Wager House.

This photograph of Harpers Ferry from the Maryland side of the Potomac shows the town as it appeared about the time of the raid. The Baltimore and Ohio Railroad bridge, by which John Brown and his raiders entered the village, is at the left.

If he so desired, he could join the Masons, the Odd Fellows, or the Sons of Temperance. Nearly everyone was prosperous. It was a good time for the town and its people.

John Brown arrived amidst this prosperity on July 3, 1859. Not yet 60 years old, the rigors of frontier living had nevertheless left their imprint upon him and there were those who said he looked and walked more than ever "like an old man." In March a Cleveland, Ohio, newspaper had described him as "a medium-sized, compactly-built and wiry man, and as quick as a cat in his movements. His hair is of a salt and pepper hue and as stiff as bristles, he has a long, waving, milk-white goatee, which gives him a somewhat patriarchal appearance, his eyes are gray and sharp." He had grown the beard before his last trip to Kansas in 1858, and it covered his square chin and straight, firm mouth, changing his appearance markedly. When he arrived in Harpers Ferry the beard had been shortened to within an inch and a half of his face, because, his daughter Annie later recalled, he thought it "more likely to disguise him than a clean face or than the long beard."

With Brown were two of his sons—34-year-old Owen and 20-year-old Oliver—and Kansas veteran Jeremiah G. Anderson. The 26-year-old, Indiana-born Anderson was the grandson of Southern slaveholders and had joined the abolitionist cause in 1857 after working several unproductive years as a peddler, farmer, and sawyer. Determined to eliminate slavery, Anderson once vowed to "make this land of liberty and equality shake to the centre."

After consulting briefly with Cook, who had been serving as a schoolteacher, book salesman, and canal-lock tender, and had even married a local girl since being sent to Harpers Ferry the year before, Brown and his three companions took up residence in a private home in Sandy Hook, a small village about a mile down the Potomac on the Maryland shore. The names they gave their landlord were "Isaac Smith & Sons." To anyone asking their business in the area, Brown told them they were simple farmers looking for good farmland to develop.

Brown arose early on July 4 and began exploring the Maryland side of the Potomac to find a suitable hideout for his raiders. Local inquiry led him to a farm owned by the heirs of a Dr. R. F. Kennedy about 5 miles north of Harpers Ferry. A cursory inspection convinced him that the place, though small, was conveniently located and admirably suited for concealment. The farm was remote from other settlements, and it was surrounded by woods and hidden by undergrowth—an ideal situation for hiding men and supplies from the gaze of inquisitive neighbors.

John Brown in May 1859.

For $35 in gold Brown rented the farm, which consisted of two log structures, some outbuildings, and a pasture. The main house sat about 100 yards off the public road connecting Harpers Ferry with Boonesborough and Sharpsburg, Md., and contained a basement kitchen and storerooms, a second-floor living room and bedrooms, and an attic. The second floor was used as kitchen, parlor, and dining room, and the attic served as a storeroom, drilling room, and "prison" to keep the men out of sight. Near the farmhouse stood a small cabin that later became a storage place and sleeping quarters for some of the raiders.

Brown's chief fear was that neighbors would become suspicious of "Isaac Smith & Sons" and possibly uncover his revolutionary plans. Reasoning that nearby families would be less distrustful with women

The isolated character of the Kennedy farm (above) did not prevent curious neighbors from "dropping in" for a visit. To help avert suspicion, Brown's daughter Annie and Oliver's wife Martha (shown here with her husband in 1859) lived at the farm while the arms and men were being assembled. Martha did the cooking and helped Annie with household chores.

among the group, he appealed to his wife and daughter Annie at their home in North Elba, N.Y., to come live with him, saying that "It will be likely to prove the most valuable service you can ever render to the world." Mrs. Brown was unable to make the long journey, but Annie and Oliver's wife Martha did join him in mid-July. Their presence proved of inestimable value not only in alleviating suspicion but in contributing to the morale of the men. Martha served as cook and housekeeper, preparing meals on a wood stove in the upstairs living room; Annie kept constant watch for prying neighbors. "When I washed dishes," noted Annie many years later,

> I stood at the end of the table where I could see out of the window and open door if any one approached the house. I was constantly on the lookout while carrying the victuals across the porch, and while I was tidying or sweeping the rooms, and always at my post on the porch when the men were eating. My evenings were spent on the porch or sitting on the stairs, watching or listening.

The Kennedy farmhouse served as the base of operations for John Brown's raiders.

Annie Brown

His base established, Brown laid plans to assemble his arms and supplies and to gather in his followers. On July 10 he wrote to John Kagi at Chambersburg, Pa., where an arms depot had been set up, giving him directions for forwarding the waiting men and the "freight"—200 Sharps rifles, an equal number of pistols, and a thousand pikes. The weapons, crated in large wooden boxes marked "Hardware and Castings," were shipped from Ohio to Chambersburg where Kagi sent them by wagon to Brown at the Kennedy farm. Supplies were acquired at various places between Chambersburg and Harpers Ferry.

Alone and in twos and threes, Brown's followers began to assemble at the farm. Watson Brown arrived on August 6. "Tall and rather fair, with finely knit frame, athletic and active," the 24-year-old Watson brought with him two of his brothers-in-law and North Elba neighbors, William and Dauphin Thompson. The Thompsons had not previously taken active roles in the anti-slavery movement but they were dedicated abolitionists.

William, 26 years old, was fun-loving and good natured. He had started for Kansas in 1856 but turned back before reaching there. His 20-year-old brother Dauphin had never been away from home before. Handsome, inexperienced, with curly, golden hair and a soft complexion, he seemed "more like a girl than a warrior" and was "diffident and quiet." Both had come to the Kennedy farm because they were firmly convinced of the justness of John Brown's cause.

Next came Aaron Stevens and Charles Plummer Tidd, a 25-year-old former Maine woodsman. Tidd was a Kansas veteran. He had been one of the first to join Brown at Tabor, Iowa, in 1857 and had remained one of his closest associates ever since. He was quick-tempered, but according to Annie Brown, "His rages soon passed and then he tried all he could to repair damages. He was a fine singer and of strong family affections."

Tidd and Stevens were followed by 22-year-old Albert Hazlett, another veteran of the Kansas fighting, Canadian-born Stewart Taylor, and two brothers from Iowa, Edwin and Barclay Coppoc. Hazlett had worked on his brother's farm in western Pennsylvania before joining Brown at the Kennedy farm. He was totally committed to the overthrow of slavery. "I am willing to die in the cause of liberty," he said; "if I had ten thousand lives I would willingly lay them all down for the same cause." Taylor, 23 years old, was once a wagonmaker. He had met Brown in Iowa in 1858 and was "heart and soul in the anti-slavery cause." Scholarly, a good debater, and "very fond of studying history," Taylor, like Stevens, was a spiritualist and had a premonition that he would die at Harpers Ferry. The Coppocs were Quakers by birth and training. They were in Kansas during the troubles there but took no part in the fighting. Edwin, at 24,

Left to right: Edwin Coppoc, Dauphin Thompson, and Charles Plummer Tidd.

was 4 years older than his brother Barclay. Both had joined Brown initially in 1858 at Springdale, Iowa, where they were living with their mother, shortly before the Chatham Convention.

Twenty-year-old William H. Leeman arrived near the end of August. Born and educated in Maine, he had worked in a Haverhill, Mass., shoe factory before going to Kansas in 1856 where he served in Brown's "Liberty Guards" militia company. Impulsive, hard to control, the 6-foot-tall Leeman "smoked a good deal and drank sometimes," but he had "a good intellect with great ingenuity." Shortly before the raid he wrote his mother that he was "warring with slavery, the greatest curse that ever infected America. We are determined to strike for freedom, incite the slaves to rebellion, and establish a free government. With the help of God we will carry it through."

After Leeman came Dangerfield Newby, a mulatto born a slave but freed by his Scotch father, and Osborn P. Anderson, a 33-year-old free Negro who had worked as a printer before joining Brown in Canada in 1858. Newby, at 44 the oldest of the group save for Brown himself, had a wife and several children in bondage in the South. He came to the Kennedy farmhouse convinced that the only way to free them was with rifle and bullet. Week after week he would read and reread a worn letter from his wife in which she begged him to "Buy me and the baby, that has just commenced to crawl, as soon as possible, for if you do not get me somebody else will."

"Emperor" Shields Green, a 23-year-old illiterate escaped slave from Charleston, S.C., joined up at Chambersburg where Brown had gone in mid-August to enlist the aid of the famed Negro abolitionist, orator, and journalist, Frederick Douglass. Brown and Douglass had first met at Springfield, Mass., in 1847. Since then they had become good friends. When the Negro leader learned the details of the planned assault on Harpers Ferry, he refused to participate, arguing that an attack on the Government would "array the whole country" against him and antagonize the very people to whom the abolitionists looked for support. Moreover, Douglass believed that the plan could not succeed, that Brown "was going into a perfect steel-trap, and that once in he would never get out alive." Before leaving, Douglass asked Shields Green, who had accompanied him to the meeting, what he intended to do. Green replied simply, "I b'lieve I'll go wid de ole man."

Life at the Kennedy farm was wearing and tedious. Brown's most trying task was to keep his slowly increasing force occupied and out of sight. Forced to remain in the two small buildings during the day, the men had little to do. The long summer days were mostly spent reading magazines, telling stories, arguing politics and religion, and playing checkers and cards. They drilled frequently and studied the art of guerrilla warfare from a specially prepared military manual.

Meals were served downstairs in the farmhouse, with Annie and Martha standing guard while the men ate. After breakfast each morning, John Brown would read from the Bible and utter a short prayer.

Occasionally he would travel into Harpers Ferry to pick up a Baltimore
newspaper to which he subscribed or to purchase flour from the mill on
Virginius Island. If a neighbor arrived unexpectedly during mealtime,
the men would gather up the food, dishes, and table cloth and carry them
to the attic.

At night the men could go outdoors for fresh air and exercise.
Thunderstorms were especially welcomed, for then they could move about
with little fear of making noise. These brief interludes served to release
tensions built up during long periods of confinement and inactivity, but
the secret living in such close quarters proved almost too much to bear.
Restiveness and irritations were bound to occur. Twice there was a near
revolt against the planned raid. On one occasion Tidd became so infuriated
that he left the farm and stayed with Cook in Harpers Ferry for 3 days.
So serious was the opposition that Brown tendered his resignation as
commander in chief. He withdrew it only after the men gave him a renewed
vote of confidence.

As September ended and the time for the attack approached, Annie
and Martha were sent back to North Elba. Brown and his men busied
themselves overhauling the rifles and pistols and attaching pike-heads to
shafts. The pikes were Brown's own idea. Preparing for a return to Kansas
in 1857, he had negotiated with a Connecticut blacksmith to manufacture
1,000 of these weapons—a two-edged dirk with an iron blade 8 inches
long fastened to a 6-foot ash handle. Originally they were intended for
the defense of free-soil settlers in Kansas, but Brown was unable to pay
for them until the spring of 1859, when he made final arrangements to use
them at Harpers Ferry. Knowing that most of the slaves he expected to
join him were unskilled in the use of firearms, he decided they could

handle a pike. A thousand men armed with pikes and backed by Brown's more experienced "soldiers" could constitute a formidable army.

Because so many people knew about Brown's intentions, it was inevitable that the secrecy would be broken. In late August Secretary of War John B. Floyd received an unsigned letter reporting "the existence of a secret association, having for its object the liberation of the slaves at the South by a general insurrection." Brown was named as its leader and "an armory in Maryland" its immediate objective. Because the informant mistakenly placed the armory in Maryland instead of Virginia and because Floyd could not bring himself to believe such a scheme could be entertained by citizens of the United States, the Secretary put the letter away and forgot about it until subsequent events reminded him of the warning.

October arrived. Still Brown delayed, hoping that more men would come. Many upon whom he had counted failed to join him for a variety of reasons. Even two of his sons, Jason and Salmon, refused to participate. Though disappointed, Brown realized that the longer he delayed, the greater were the chances that his plan would be discovered and thwarted. Finally, on October 15, with the arrival of 22-year-old Francis J. Meriam and two Ohio Negroes, John Copeland and Lewis S. Leary, both 25, the ranks of the "Provisional Army of the United States" were completed. In all there were 21 men besides the commander in chief. Of these, 19 were under 30, three not yet 21. Brown could wait no longer. Calling his men together, he announced that the attack would take place the next night, October 16, and cautioned them about the needless taking of human life:

> You all know how dear life is to you . . . consider that the lives of others are as dear to them as yours are to you; do not, therefore, take the life of anyone if you can possibly avoid it, but if it is necessary to take life in order to save your own, then make short work of it.

TO FREE THE SLAVES

The daylight hours of Sunday, October 16, 1859, were quiet ones at the Kennedy farm as the long period of inactivity and uncertainty neared its climax. Early in the morning John Brown held worship services, the impending attack invoking "deep solemnity" upon the gathering. After breakfast and roll call a final meeting was held and instructions were given. Then everything was in readiness.

About 8 p.m. Brown turned to his followers. "Men," he said, "get on your arms; we will proceed to the Ferry." The men, ready for hours, slung their Sharps rifles over their shoulders, concealing them under long, gray shawls that served as overcoats, and waited for the order to march. A horse and wagon were brought to the door of the farmhouse. In the wagon the men placed a few items that might be needed for the work ahead: a sledge hammer, a crowbar, and several pikes. Owen Brown, Barclay Coppoc, and Meriam were detailed to remain at the farm as a rearguard.

In the morning they were to bring the rest of the weapons nearer the town where they could be passed out to the slave army Brown expected to raise.

Donning his battered old Kansas cap, symbol of the violence to which he had contributed in that strife-torn territory, Brown mounted the wagon and motioned his men to move out. From the farmhouse the group moved down the lane and onto the road leading to Harpers Ferry. Tidd and Cook, who were best acquainted with the route, preceded the main body as scouts. Upon reaching the town they were to cut the telegraph lines on both the Maryland and Virginia sides of the Potomac.

Francis J. Meriam

Owen Brown

Barclay Coppoc

Brown used this schoolhouse near Harpers Ferry as an arsenal after the raid began. The drawing was made about 1859 by David Hunter Strother, known to readers of Harper's New Monthly Magazine as "Porte Crayon," one of the most popular illustrators of mid-19th century America.

For more than 2 hours the men tramped along behind the wagon, strictly adhering to Brown's order to maintain silence. About 10:30 p.m. they reached the Baltimore and Ohio Railroad bridge that would carry them into Harpers Ferry. It was a long wooden-covered structure that spanned the Potomac River a little upstream from where the Shenandoah comes spilling in from the south. Kagi and Stevens entered first and encountered watchman William Williams, who approached with a lantern. They quickly took Williams prisoner. The rest of the raiders, except for Watson Brown and Stewart Taylor who were told to stay on the Maryland side as a rearguard, fastened cartridges boxes to the outside of their clothing for ready access and followed the wagon onto the bridge.

Crossing quickly, the raiders stepped from the tunnel's black throat into the slumbering town. Before them lay a large structure that doubled as the railroad depot and the Wager House. Just beyond, to the left, was the U.S. Arsenal buildings where thousands of guns were stored. To the right the armory shops stretched in a double row along the Potomac. Brown turned the horse and wagon toward the armory.

Daniel Whelan, the armory's nightwatchman, heard the wagon coming down the street from the depot. Thinking it was the head watchman, he came out from his station in the fire enginehouse (a one-story, two-room brick building that doubled as a guard post just inside the armory grounds) to find several rifles pointed at him. "Open the gate!" someone yelled. Out of sheer cussedness, or perhaps fright, Whelan refused. One of the raiders took the crowbar from the wagon and twisted it in the chain until the lock snapped. The gate was thrown open and the wagon rolled into the yard. To his prisoners, Whelan and Williams, Brown announced his purpose:

I came here from Kansas, and this is a slave state; I want to free all the Negroes in this state; I have possession now of the United States armory, and if the citizens interfere with me I must only burn the town and have blood.

Once in control of the armory, Brown detailed his men to other objectives. Oliver Brown and William Thompson were sent to watch the bridge across the Shenandoah River, while Hazlett and Edwin Coppoc moved into the unguarded arsenal. Another group of raiders under Stevens made its way down Shenandoah Street to the rifle factory on Lower Hall Island. Again the watchman was surprised and easily captured. Telling Kagi and Copeland to watch the rifle works—Leary would join them later—Stevens marched the watchman and several young men picked up on the street back to the armory grounds.

So far Brown's occupation of the town had been quiet and peaceful. It did not last. About midnight another watchman, Patrick Higgins, a Sandy Hook resident, arrived at the Maryland end of the B & O bridge to relieve Williams. Finding the structure dark he called out loudly; he was answered quietly by Taylor and Watson Brown, who took him prisoner. As he was being escorted across the bridge, Higgins suddenly lashed out, struck Brown in the face, and raced toward the town. Taylor fired after him. The ball grazed the watchman's scalp, but he reached the Wager House safely. The first shot of the raid had been fired.

About this same time Stevens led several raiders on a special mission to capture Col. Lewis W. Washington, the 46-year-old great-grandnephew of George Washington. The colonel, a small but prosperous planter, lived near Halltown just off the Charles Town Turnpike about 5 miles west of Harpers Ferry. He owned a pistol presented to General Washington by the Marquis de Lafayette and a sword reportedly presented by the Prussian King Frederick the Great. Brown wanted these weapons. When he struck the first blow to free the slaves he rather fancied the idea of wearing the sword and brandishing the pistol once owned by the man who had led the fight to free the American colonists from a similar kind of tyranny.

Battering down Washington's door, Stevens, Tidd, Cook, and three Negroes—Anderson, Leary, and Green—summoned the colonel from his bed. Washington offered no resistance. Calmly surrendering the sword and pistol, he then dressed and climbed into his carriage for the trip to Harpers Ferry. The raiders and Washington's three slaves crammed into the colonel's four-horse farm wagon and followed along behind the carriage.

"Beallair," the home of Col. Lewis Washington.
Late on the night of October 16, several raiders broke
into this house in search of a pistol and sword
once owned by the colonel's great grand-
uncle, George Washington. Colonel Washington
(inset) was taken hostage.

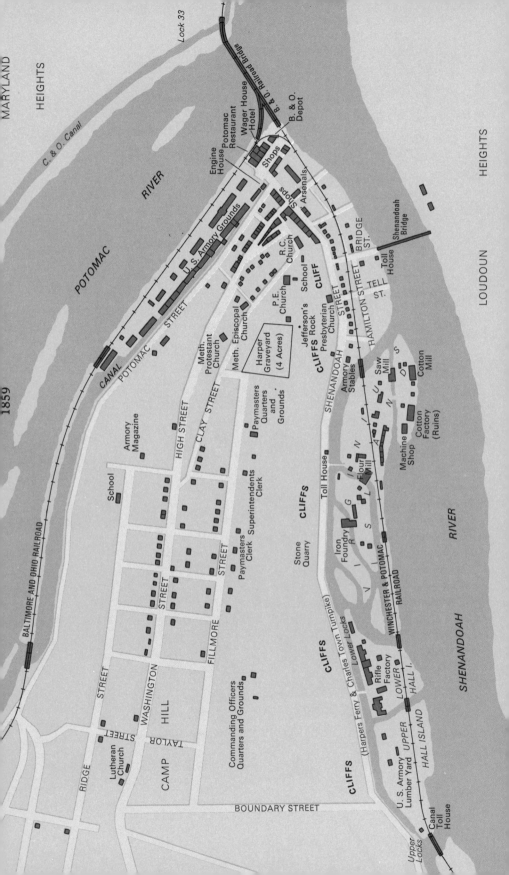

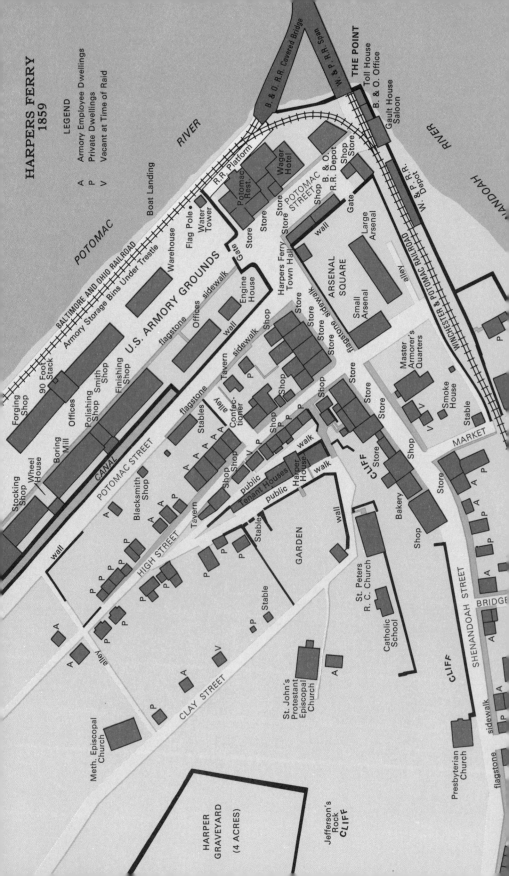

HARPERS FERRY
1859

LEGEND

A Armory Employee Dwellings
P Private Dwellings
V Vacant at Time of Raid

POTOMAC   RIVER

B. & O. R.R. Covered Bridge

W. & P. R.R. Span

THE POINT

Toll House

B. & O. Office

Gault House Saloon

BALTIMORE AND OHIO RAILROAD

Armory Storage Bins Under Trestle

Boat Landing

Warehouse

Flag Pole

Water Tower

Gate

Gate

R.R. Platform

Potomac Rest.

Wager Hotel

Store

Store

Store

POTOMAC STREET

Store

Store

Shop

B. & O. R.R. Depot

Store

Gate

Large Arsenal

W. & P. R.R. Depot

U.S. ARMORY GROUNDS

flagstone

Offices

sidewalk

wall

Engine House

Harpers Ferry Town Hall

wall

ARSENAL SQUARE

Small Arsenal

alley

Forging Shop

90 Foot Stack

Offices

Polishing Shop

Finishing Shop

Smith Shop

Boring Mill

CANAL

POTOMAC STREET

flagstone

Tavern

sidewalk

Confectioner

Shop

Shop

Shop

P

Shop

Shop

Store

Store

sidewalk

sidewalk

flagstone

Store

Store

Store

Master Armorer's Quarters

Smoke House

Stable

WINCHESTER & POTOMAC RAILROAD

Stocking Shop

Wheel House

Blacksmith Shop

Stables

Shop

A

A

A

A

A

alley

A

A

P

P

P

Tavern

Shop

P

P

P

P

V

Shop

P

Store

Store

Shop

V

V

V

P

MARKET

wall

HIGH STREET

Tavern

P

P

P

P

P

P

A

A

P

P

Harper Tenant Houses

public

public

walk

walk

Harper House

public

walk

Store

Store

CLIFF

Bakery

Shop

Store

Store

A

P

P

A

A

P

P

P

Meth. Episcopal Church

A

A

P

P

P

P

P

Stable

Stable

GARDEN

wall

St. Peters R. C. Church

Catholic School

Shop

Store

A

A

P

A

P

P

SHENANDOAH STREET

BRIDGE

CLIFF

St. John's Protestant Episcopal Church

V

A

A

CLAY STREET

P

Presbyterian Church

sidewalk

flagstone

A

P

HARPER GRAVEYARD

(4 ACRES)

Jefferson's Rock CLIFF

POTOMAC   RIVER

SHENANDOAH   RIVER

On the way the procession stopped at the home of another slaveholder, John Allstadt, just west of Bolivar Heights. Again using a fence rail to gain entrance, the raiders forced Allstadt and his 18-year-old son into the wagon while the terror-stricken women of the house shrieked "Murder!" from the upstairs windows. Allstadt's four slaves were also added to the group.

While Stevens' party was gathering hostages, the first note of tragedy was sounded. At 1:25 a.m. the Baltimore and Ohio passenger train eastbound for Baltimore arrived at Harpers Ferry and was stopped by a clerk from the Wager House who told conductor A. J. Phelps of the recent "startling" events. Phelps refused to allow the train to cross the bridge until it had been checked, and he sent engineer William McKay and baggagemaster Jacob Cromwell out to investigate. They were halted by Brown's guards, who turned them back at gunpoint.

Hayward Shepherd, the station baggageman, heard the commotion and walked out to see what was going on. Shepherd, a free Negro, was highly respected and well-liked by all who knew him. As he approached the bridge a raider told him to halt. Instead, Shepherd turned around and started back toward the station. A shot rang out and he fell gravely wounded. He dragged himself back to the station where he died the next afternoon. The first person to die at the hands of the men who had come to free the slaves was, in fact, a Negro already free.

Between 4 and 5 a.m. the caravan containing Colonel Washington and the Allstadts arrived at the armory. Brown armed the frightened slaves with pikes and told them to guard the prisoners, who were placed in the enginehouse and now numbered about a half-dozen. "Keep these white men inside," he said. Turning to Washington, Brown explained that he had

"Porte Crayon's" drawing of Hayward Shepherd, the free Negro baggageman killed by one of Brown's men on October 17, is the only known portrait of this tragic figure.

Brown kept his growing number of hostages in the fire enginehouse at left, just inside the entrance to the U.S. Armory grounds. The machine shops where the muskets were assembled are at the right.

taken him hostage because "as the aid to the Governor of Virginia, I knew you would endeavor to perform your duty, and perhaps you would have been a troublesome customer to me; and, apart from that, I wanted you particularly for the moral effect it would give our cause, having one of your name our prisoner." As dawn approached the number of Brown's prisoners increased as unsuspecting armory employees reporting for work were seized as they passed through the gate. Perhaps as many as 40 hostages were eventually jammed into the two rooms of the enginehouse.

Near dawn, John Cook, with two raiders and a handful of pike-carrying Negroes, took the wagon across the bridge into Maryland to bring the weapons closer to the town to arm the hundreds of slaves soon expected to join the fight. The rest of Brown's "army" settled down at their posts in the waning darkness to await the coming of day, the last for many of them.

Thus far the citizens of Harpers Ferry had offered no resistance to the invasion of their town, primarily because most of the townspeople knew nothing of what was taking place. At the first streak of daylight, Dr. John Starry, a 35-year-old local physician who had maintained an all-night vigil beside the dying Hayward Shepherd, began to alert the people to the danger. After arousing the residents of Virginius Island, he rode to warn Acting Armory Superintendent A. M. Kitzmiller. Next he ordered the Lutheran Church bell rung to assemble the citizens and ascertain what arms were available for defense. Then he sent a messenger off to Shepherdstown and another to Charles Town to alert their militia companies of the armed occupation of Harpers Ferry.

Among the townspeople there were only one or two squirrel rifles and a few shotguns, none of which were really fit for use. All other weapons were in the arsenal buildings, and they were occupied by the raiders. Knowing it would be futile to confront Brown's men unarmed, Dr. Starry headed for Charles Town, 8 miles away, to hurry its militia along. But no prompting was necessary. To Charles Town residents the news from Harpers Ferry was frightening, for it awakened memories of the 1831 Nat Turner slave rebellion in Virginia's tidewater region when more than 50 whites, mostly women and children, were murdered before the bloody uprising was put down. The Jefferson Guards and another hastily formed company would march as soon as possible.

At daylight on October 17 Brown allowed the B & O passenger train to continue its journey to Baltimore. Conductor Phelps wasted no time in sounding the alarm. At Monocacy, Md., at 7:05 a.m. he telegraphed his superiors about the night's events, adding:

They say they have come to free the slaves and intend to do it

*at all hazards. The leader of those men requested me to say to
you that this is the last train that shall pass the bridge either East
or West. If it is attempted it will be at the peril of the lives of
those having them in charge. . . . It has been suggested you had
better notify the Secretary of War at once. The telegraph lines are
cut East and West of Harper's Ferry and this is the first station
that I could send a dispatch from.*

John W. Garrett, president of the railroad, saw the message when it came
in and immediately sent word to President James Buchanan and Virginia
Governor Henry A. Wise. At the same time he alerted Maj. Gen. George
H. Stewart, commanding Baltimore's First Light Division of the Maryland
Volunteers. Word was also flashed to Frederick, Md., and that town's
militia was soon under arms.

By 7 a.m. the residents of Harpers Ferry had discovered a supply of
guns in a building overlooked by the raiders, and some of the townspeople
began to move against Brown and his men. Alexander Kelly, armed with
a shotgun, approached the corner of High and Shenandoah Streets, about
100 yards from the armory. Before he could fire, several bullets whizzed
past his head, one putting a hole through his hat. Shortly afterwards,
groceryman Thomas Boerly, a man of great physical strength and
courage, approached the same corner and opened fire on a group of
Brown's men standing in the arsenal yard, diagonally across the street
from the armory gate. A return bullet knocked him down with a "ghastly"
wound, from which he soon died.

A lull followed the shooting of Boerly. Brown, having made no
provision to feed his men and hostages, released Walter Kemp, an infirm
Wager House bartender captured earlier, in exchange for 45 breakfasts.
But when the food came, few ate it. Many, including Washington, Allstadt,
and Brown himself, feared it had been drugged or poisoned.

Meanwhile, Kagi, still at the rifle factory, was anxiously sending
messages to Brown urging him to leave Harpers Ferry while they still had
the chance. Brown ignored the pleas and continued to direct operations
with no apparent thought that outside forces would be moving against him
once the alarm had spread. Why, is anybody's guess. Up until noon of
October 17, despite the erratic fire from the townspeople, the raiders could
have fought their way to safety in the mountains. Instead, Brown waited,
doing nothing. By mid-day it was too late, and the jaws of the "steel-trap"
foreseen by Frederick Douglass closed swiftly.

THE TIGER CAGED

The Charles Town militia, consisting of the regular company of the
Jefferson Guards and a specially formed volunteer company, was armed
and on its way by train to Harpers Ferry by 10 a.m. The militia
commander, Col. John T. Gibson, had not waited for orders from
Richmond but had set out as soon as the men could be gotten ready.

William Thompson

Watson Brown

Arriving at Halltown, about midway between Charles Town and Harpers Ferry, Gibson, fearing the track ahead might be torn up, took the militia off the train and marched by road to Allstadt's Crossroads west of Bolivar Heights.

At Allstadt's, Gibson divided his force. He sent Mexican War veteran Capt. J. W. Rowan with the Jefferson Guards in a wide sweep to the west of Harpers Ferry to capture the B & O bridge. Gibson himself would take the volunteer company on into town. Rowan's men crossed the Potomac about a mile above Harpers Ferry and, advancing along the towpath of the Chesapeake and Ohio Canal, arrived at the Maryland end of the bridge by noon. With little difficulty they drove its defenders—Oliver Brown, William Thompson, and Dangerfield Newby—back toward the armory yard. Only Brown and Thompson made it. Newby, the ex-slave who had joined John Brown to free his wife and children, was killed by a 6-inch spike fired from a smoothbore musket. He was the first of the raiders to die.

In the meantime, Colonel Gibson's force had arrived in Harpers Ferry and he sent a detachment of citizens under Capt. Lawson Botts, a Charles Town attorney, to secure the Gault House Saloon at the rear of the arsenal and commanding the Shenandoah bridge and the entrance to the armory yard. Another detachment under Capt. John Avis, the Charles Town jailer, took up positions in houses along Shenandoah Street from which to fire into the arsenal grounds.

The attack of the Charles Town militia cut off Brown's escape route and separated him from his men in Maryland and those still holding the rifle factory. At last, perhaps realizing the hopelessness of his situation, Brown sought a truce. But when hostage Rezin Cross and raider William

Thompson emerged from the enginehouse under a white flag, the townspeople ignored the flag, seized Thompson, and dragged him off to the Wager House where he was kept under guard.

Still not convinced, Brown tried again. This time he sent his son Watson and Aaron Stevens with Acting Armory Superintendent Kitzmiller, taken hostage earlier in the day. As the trio marched onto the street and came opposite the Galt House, several shots rang out and both raiders fell. Stevens, severely wounded, lay bleeding in the street; Watson Brown, mortally wounded, dragged himself back to the enginehouse. Joseph Brua, one of the hostages, volunteered to aid the wounded Stevens. As bullets richocheted off the flagstone walk, Brua walked out, lifted up the wounded raider, and carried him to the Wager House for medical attention. Then, incredibly, he strolled back to the enginehouse and again took his place among Brown's prisoners. Kitzmiller escaped.

About the time Stevens and Watson Brown were shot, raider William Leeman attempted to escape. Dashing through the upper end of the armory yard, he plunged into the frigid Potomac, comparatively shallow at this point, and made for the Maryland shore. Soon spotted, a shower of bullets hit the water around him and he was forced to take refuge on an islet in the river. G. A. Schoppert, a Harpers Ferry resident, waded out to where Leeman lay marooned, pointed a pistol at his head, and pulled the trigger. For the rest of the day Leeman's body was a target for the undisciplined militia and townspeople.

Oliver Brown, William Thompson, and Dangerfield Newby were forced to abandon their post at the Maryland end of the Baltimore and Ohio Railroad bridge when they were attacked by the Jefferson Guards. Brown and Thompson reached the armory grounds safely, but Newby (inset) was shot and killed as he came off the bridge.

When a raider shot and killed George W. Turner about 2 p.m., the crowd grew ugly. Turner, a West Point graduate, was a prominent and highly respected area planter. When Fontaine Beckham, the mayor of Harpers Ferry and agent for the B & O Railroad, was killed, the townspeople turned into a howling, raging mob.

Beckham, a well-liked man of somewhat high-strung temperament, had been greatly disturbed by the earlier shooting of Hayward Shepherd, his friend and faithful helper at the depot. Despite warnings from friends to keep away, Beckham, unarmed, walked out on the railroad to see what was going on. He paced up and down the B & O trestle bordering the armory yard about 30 yards from the enginehouse. Several raiders spotted him peering around the water tower in front of their stronghold and thought that he was placing himself in position to fire through the doors. Edwin Coppoc, posted at the doorway of the enginehouse, leveled his rifle at the mayor.

"Don't fire, man, for God's sake!" screamed one of the hostages. "They'll shoot in here and kill us all."

Coppoc ignored the warning and pulled the trigger. Beckham fell, a bullet through his heart. Oliver Brown, standing beside Coppoc in the partly opened doorway, aimed his rifle at another man on the trestle, but before he could fire he keeled over with "a mortal wound that gave horrible pain." Both of Brown's sons now lay dying at their father's feet.

Enraged by the shooting of Beckham, the townspeople turned on prisoner William Thompson. Led by Harry Hunter, a young Charles Town volunteer and the grandnephew of the murdered mayor, a group of men stormed into the Wager House, grabbed Thompson, and dragged him out onto the B & O bridge. "You may kill me but it will be revenged," Thompson yelled; "there are eighty thousand persons sworn to carry out this work." These were his last words. The mob shot him several times and tossed his body into the Potomac to serve, like Leeman's, as a target for the remainder of the day.

While Brown's situation at the fire enginehouse was growing progressively worse, his three-man detachment holding the rifle works came under fire. Under Kagi's leadership these men had held the works uncontested during the morning and early afternoon. About 2:30 p.m. Dr. Starry organized a party of "citizens and neighbors" and launched an attack against the raiders from Shenandoah Street. After a brief exchange of shots, Kagi, Lewis Leary, and John Copeland dashed out the back of the building, scrambled across the Winchester and Potomac Railroad tracks, and waded into the shallow Shenandoah River. Some townspeople posted on the opposite bank spotted the fleeing men and opened fire. The raiders, caught in a crossfire, made for a large flat rock in the middle of the river. Kagi, Brown's most trusted and able lieutenant, was killed in the attempt and Leary was mortally wounded.

Copeland reached the rock only to be dragged ashore, where the excited crowd screamed "Lynch him! Lynch him!" But Dr. Starry intervened, and the frightened Negro was hustled off to jail.

At the enginehouse, the raiders continued to exchange occasional shots with the Charles Town militia and the townspeople. By now Brown had separated his prisoners. Eleven of the more important hostages who might be used for bargaining purposes were moved into the engineroom with his dwindling band, while the others remained crowded into the tiny guardroom. The two rooms were separated by a solid brick wall.

Lewis S. Leary

William H. Leeman

About 3 p.m., shortly after the raiders were driven out of the rifle works, a militia company arrived by train from Martinsburg, Va. Headed by Capt. E. G. Alburtis and comprised mostly of B & O Railroad employees, this company marched on the enginehouse from the upper end of the armory yard and came close to ending the raid. Brown positioned his men in front of the building to meet the attack. Alburtis' contingent, advancing briskly and maintaining a steady fire, forced the raiders back inside. Smashing the windows of the guardroom, the militiamen freed the prisoners but were forced to withdraw after eight of their number were wounded from the constant fire pouring from the partly opened enginehouse door. Alburtis later complained that had his men been supported by the other militia companies present, John Brown's raid would have been ended.

Other militia units now began to arrive. Between 3 and 4 p.m. the Hamtramck Guards and the Shepherdstown Troop, both from Shepherdstown, Va., came in. At dusk three uniformed companies from Frederick, Md., appeared, followed later in the evening by a Winchester, Va., company under R. B. Washington, and five companies of the Maryland Volunteers under General Stewart from Baltimore. None of them made any attempt to dislodge Brown and his men from the enginehouse, but all added to the general confusion and hysteria gripping the town.

The attack on the enginehouse by Baltimore and Ohio Railroad employees led by Capt. E. G. Alburtis is shown in this contemporary engraving from Frank Leslie's Illustrated Newspaper. *Alburtis'* attack failed to dislodge the raiders, but his men did manage to free several of Brown's hostages.

W.C.STEPHENS

On the other side of the Potomac, Cook, Owen Brown, Barclay Coppoc, Meriam, Tidd, and several Negroes had been transferring weapons to a tiny schoolhouse midway between Harpers Ferry and the Kennedy farm. As the day wore on and the firing from town became heavier, they began to suspect that something might have gone wrong. At about 4 p.m. Cook headed for the B & O bridge to see what was happening. To get a better vantage point, he climbed the craggy face of Maryland Heights where he could look directly into the center of the town. Seeing that his compatriots were "completely surrounded," he decided to try to take some of the pressure off by firing across the river at men posted in the houses along High Street overlooking the armory. His shot was instantly answered by a volley of bullets that severed a branch he was clutching for support and sent him tumbling down the rocky cliff. Badly cut and bruised from the fall, he limped back to the schoolhouse and joined the others. Realizing there was nothing they could do to aid their comrades trapped in the enginehouse, they reluctantly gathered their belongings, climbed the mountain and headed north.

Stewart Taylor

John A. Copeland

Jeremiah G. Anderson

Time was quickly running out for John Brown. As resistance became partially organized at Harpers Ferry, steps were taken to seal off any possibility of support reaching the raiders. Fearing that Brown's raid might be part of a general uprising, all approaches to the town were guarded, and all travelers not familiar to residents of the area were immediately arrested and shipped off to the county jail at Charles Town.

As night approached, the firing sputtered out. Brown, knowing escape was impossible, again attempted to bargain for freedom. In verbal and written pleas he offered to release his hostages if he and his men were allowed to leave unmolested. Col. Robert W. Taylor, now commanding the Virginia militia units at Harpers Ferry, rejected the offers, sending back word that if the prisoners were immediately released he would let the Government deal with Brown and his men. But the old abolitionist would not yield, and prisoners, slaves, and raiders alike settled down, as best they could, to what would be a long and depressing night.

Brown paced up and down like a caged tiger. It had been hours since he or any of them had tasted food or drink. The cold night air chilled their bones and the pungent odor of gunpowder stung their nostrils. The large-scale slave support that he had counted upon and for which the pikes were intended had not materialized. This was largely his own doing, however, for in his desire for absolute secrecy he had given no advance word that he was coming. The slaves had no idea that a raid was in progress. The few his men had picked up at the Washington and Allstadt farms were of no use to him. They were frightened and preferred to remain with the white hostages rather than take an active part in their own salvation. Most likely they would not have joined him at all had they not been taken from their homes at gunpoint.

From time to time Brown called out, "Men, are you awake?" Only five of the raiders were still unwounded and able to hold a rifle: Brown himself, Edwin Coppoc, J. G. Anderson, Dauphin Thompson, and Shields Green. Stewart Taylor, the Canadian soldier of fortune, lay dead in a corner, his presentiment of death come true. He had been shot like Oliver Brown while standing at the enginehouse doorway. Oliver himself, writhing in pain, begged to be killed and put out of his misery. "If you must die, then die like a man," snapped his father. After awhile Oliver was quiet. "I guess he is dead," Brown said. Nearby, Watson Brown lay quietly breathing his last. The attack that had begun but 24 hours before was fast coming to an end.

THE TRAP IS SPRUNG

The somberness that permeated the fire enginehouse contrasted sharply with the din outside. Hundreds of militiamen and townspeople jammed the streets, which echoed with whoops and yells. Anxious and hysterical friends and relatives of Brown's hostages added to the confusion. While the quasi-military operations ended at nightfall, the non-military activities

Osborn P. Anderson

continued with increasing fervor. The bars in the Wager House and Gault House Saloon were enjoying an unprecedented business. Many men were intoxicated, and they fired their guns wildly into the air and occasionally at the enginehouse. All semblance of order was gone and the "wildest excitement" prevailed throughout the night.

During this confusion two of Brown's men made their escape. Of the raiders caught in Harpers Ferry when the Jefferson Guards seized the B & O bridge at midday on October 17, Albert Hazlett and Osborn P. Anderson, occupying the arsenal, went unnoticed during the day. At night they crept out, mingled with the disorderly crowds, crossed the Potomac into Maryland, and fled north.

Into the midst of the chaos created by the drunken and disorderly militia and townspeople marched 90 U.S. Marines led by a 52-year-old Army colonel, Robert E. Lee. Lee had been at his home in Arlington, Va., that afternoon when Lt. J. E. B. Stuart brought him secret orders to report to the War Department at once. There President Buchanan and Secretary of War Floyd told him of Brown's attack and ordered him to leave immediately for Harpers Ferry with the only Federal troops readily available, a detachment of Marines at the Washington Navy Yard. Upon his arrival at Harpers Ferry, Lee was to take command of all forces in the town. Lieutenant Stuart, scenting excitement, asked for and received permission to accompany Lee, who, in the hurry of departure, had no time to return home and don his uniform.

The Marines, under the immediate command of Lt. Israel Green, left Washington before Lee and arrived at Sandy Hook in late afternoon. Lee and Stuart joined them at 10:30 p.m. Marching into Harpers Ferry, the Marines entered the armory yard about 11 p.m. and replaced the disorganized militia. Lee would have ordered an immediate attack on the enginehouse "But for the fear of sacrificing the lives of some of the gentlemen held . . . as prisoners . . . ."

About 2:30 a.m., October 18, Lee wrote a surrender demand and handed it to Stuart for delivery to Brown under a white flag when so directed. He hoped that the raider chieftain could be persuaded to surrender peaceably and avoid further bloodshed, but he expected that he would be taken only by force and laid his plans accordingly. In the early morning hours, Lee, believing the raid to be chiefly aimed against State authority and not the Federal Government, offered the honor of assaulting the enginehouse to Colonel Shriver of the Maryland Volunteers. Shriver declined. "These men of mine have wives and children," he said. "I will not expose them to such risks. You are paid for doing this kind of work." Lee then offered the task to Colonel Baylor of the Virginia militia. Baylor promptly declined it for the same reasons. Lieutenant Green was then asked if he wished "the honor of taking those men out." Green lifted his cap, thanked Lee, and picked a storming party of 12 men. He instructed them to use only their bayonets, as bullets might injure some of the hostages.

Trapped inside the armory enginehouse, the raiders and their hostages await the attack by U.S. Marines under Col. Robert E. Lee.

By 7 a.m. there was enough light for operations. All arrangements for the assault had been completed. The militia formed up outside the armory wall to keep the street clear of spectators and to prevent indiscriminate firing that might injure the storming party. The Marines took position at the northwest corner of the enginehouse, just out of the line of fire from the door. Then Lieutenant Stuart moved forward with the surrender demand. Brown opened the door a few inches and placed his body against the crack so the lieutenant could not see inside. He held a cocked rifle in one hand. Stuart read the terms offered by Lee:

Colonel Lee, United States Army, commanding troops sent by the President of the United States to suppress the insurrection at this place, demands the surrender of the persons in the Armory buildings. If they will peaceably surrender themselves and restore the pillaged property, they shall be kept in safety to await the orders of the President. Col. Lee represents to them, in all frankness, that it is impossible for them to escape; that the Armory is surrounded on all sides by troops; and that if he is compelled to take them by force he cannot answer for their safety.

Robert E. Lee (left) and J. E. B. Stuart are pictured here about the time of the raid. This little-known portrait of Stuart shows him in civilian dress and with trimmed beard.

According to Stuart, the parley was "a long one." Brown refused to surrender. Instead he presented his own propositions "in every possible shape, and with admirable tact," insisting that he, his men, and his hostages be permitted to cross the river unmolested.

Stuart, instructed not to accept any counter-proposals, sensed that further discussion was useless. Stepping back from the door, he waved his hat, a pre-arranged signal for the Marines to attack. Brown slammed the

Lt. Israel Green (right) led the Marine attack on the enginehouse and was the first man to enter the building. The engraving below shows the Marines battering the enginehouse door while under fire from raiders inside.

door shut and the troops came on. Three men with sledge hammers pounded the center door of the enginehouse, but it would not yield; the raiders had placed the fire engines against it. Spotting a heavy ladder nearby, Lieutenant Green directed his men to use it as a battering-ram. On the second blow the door splintered and a small opening was effected.

Lieutenant Green was the first man through. Maj. W. W. Russell, armed only with a rattan cane, followed immediately. Pvt. Luke Quinn squeezed through behind Russell and fell dead at the door, shot through his groin. Another Marine, Pvt. Mathew Ruppert, stepped over Quinn, then dropped his gun and clawed his face in pain where a bullet had torn through his cheek. The rest of the storming party entered without injury.

The hostages cowered at the rear of the building; Brown knelt between the fire engines, rifle in hand. As Green came through the row of engines, Colonel Washington greeted him and pointed at Brown. Green raised his sword and brought it down with all his strength, cutting a deep wound in the back of the raider chieftain's neck. As Brown fell, Green lunged with his sword, striking part of the raider's accouterments and bending the blade double. Green then showered blow after blow upon Brown's head until he fell unconscious. Two of the raiders were killed almost immediately after the Marines entered the building: Dauphin Thompson, pinned against the rear wall by a bayonet, and Jeremiah Anderson, run through by a saber as he sought refuge under one of the fire engines. Edwin Coppoc and Shields Green surrendered. The fight was over in about 3 minutes.

After their capture, Brown and his surviving men were placed under guard outside the enginehouse, where they were subjected to taunts and threats of angry militia and townspeople.

None of the hostages was injured, although Lieutenant Green considered them the "sorriest lot of people I ever saw." The dead, dying, and wounded raiders were carried outside and laid in a row on the grass. As Brown slowly regained consciousness, the Marines had trouble keeping back the throngs of militia and townspeople who wanted to see the wounded raider leader. After noon, Brown and Stevens, still suffering from the wounds he received on October 17, were carried to the paymaster's office where a group of inquisitors, including Virginia's Governor Henry A. Wise and Senator James M. Mason, and Ohio Congressman Clement L. Vallandigham, questioned them for 3 hours in an effort to learn their purpose and the names of their supporters in the North.

During the interrogation Brown lay on the floor, his hair matted and tangled, his face, hands, and clothes soiled and smeared with blood. He talked freely, and while he readily admitted his intention to free the slaves, "and only that," he refused to divulge the names of his Northern backers. "No man sent me here," he said; "it was my own prompting and that of my Maker, or that of the devil, whichever you ascribe it to. I *acknowledge no man in human form."* He continued:

I want you to understand, gentlemen . . . that I respect the rights of the poorest and weakest of colored people, oppressed by the slave system, just as much as I do those of the most wealthy and powerful. That is the idea that has moved me, and that alone. We expect no reward, except the satisfaction of endeavoring to do for those in distress and greatly oppressed, as we would be done by. The cry of distress of the oppressed is my reason, and the only thing that has prompted me to come here.

Brown then issued a prophetic warning:

I wish to say furthermore, that you had better—all you people at the South—prepare yourselves for a settlement of that question that must come up for settlement sooner than you are prepared for it. The sooner you are prepared the better. You may dispose of me very easily; I am nearly disposed of now; but this question is still to be settled—this negro question I mean—the end of that is not yet.

JOHN BROWN'S BODY

The day after their capture, Brown and his surviving followers—Stevens, Edwin Coppoc, Shields Green, and John Copeland—were taken to Charles Town under heavy guard and lodged in the county jail. The cell doors had hardly banged shut when they learned that they were to receive speedy trials. The grand jury was then in session, and the semiannual term of the circuit court, presided over by Judge Richard Parker, had begun.

The five raiders were arraigned on October 25, just one week after their capture. The next day they were indicted for treason against the Commonwealth of Virginia, for conspiring with slaves to rebel, and for murder. Each defendant pleaded "Not guilty" and each asked for a separate trial. The court consented and elected to try Brown first. Two court-appointed attorneys, 36-year-old Lawson Botts, who had helped to capture the raiders, and Thomas C. Green, the 39-year-old Mayor of Charles Town, were called upon to defend him. Charles Harding, Commonwealth Attorney for Jefferson County, and Andrew Hunter, a veteran Charles Town lawyer, served as prosecutors for the State.

The trial began on October 27. It lasted 3½ days. Still suffering from his wounds, Brown was carried back and forth from jail to courthouse, and lay on a cot during much of the proceedings. Judge Parker had hardly brought the court to order when defense counsel Botts astounded the packed courtroom (including Brown himself) by reading a telegram from A. H. Lewis of Akron, Ohio, dated October 26:

John Brown, leader of the insurrection at Harper's Ferry, and several of his family, have resided in this county for many years. Insanity is hereditary in that family. His mother's sister died with it, and a

John Brown was tried in the courthouse at Charles Town, about 10 miles from Harpers Ferry. The trial was presided over by the Hon. Richard Parker (inset), circuit judge for Jefferson County.

*daughter of that sister has been two years in a Lunatic Asylum. A son
and daughter of his mother's brother have also been confined in the
lunatic asylum, and another son of that brother is now insane and
under close restraint. These facts can be conclusively proven by
witnesses residing here, who will doubtless attend the trial if desired.*

After receiving the telegram, Botts had gone to the jail to talk with Brown
about it. The raider leader had readily admitted that there were instances
of insanity in his mother's side of the family (in fact, his mother had died
insane), but asserted that there was none at all on his father's side. He
said his first wife had shown symptoms of it, as had two of their sons,
Frederick and John, Jr. Clearly, by introducing the Lewis telegram, the
defense hoped to save Brown's life by having him declared insane and
committed to an institution. But the old abolitionist refused to sanction
such a plea. Rising up on his cot, he exclaimed:

*I will add, if the Court will allow me, that I look upon it as a
miserable artifice and pretext of those who ought to take a different
course in regard to me, if they took any at all, and I view it with
contempt more than otherwise. As I remarked to Mr. Green, insane
persons, so far as my experience goes, have but little ability to judge
of their own sanity; and, if I am insane, of course I should think
I know more than all the rest of the world. But I do not think so. I am
perfectly unconscious of insanity, and I reject, so far as I am capable,
any attempt to interfere in my behalf on that score.*

*Lawson Botts (left) and Thomas C. Green were appointed
by the court to defend the raider leader. Brown, however,
did not trust them to provide him an adequate defense.*

Brown had more faith in the three lawyers provided by his Northern friends. Clockwise from left: George Hoyt, shown here as an officer during the Civil War, Samuel Chilton, and Hiram Griswold. Their efforts to save him from the gallows, however, proved fruitless.

Judge Parker ruled out the insanity plea on the basis that the evidence had not been presented in a reliable form. He also rejected Bott's request for a delay in the proceedings to allow new counsel of Brown's own choosing to come from Ohio. The trial continued.

The defense lawyers were increased to three when George Hoyt joined Botts and Green. Hoyt, a 21-year-old Boston lawyer, was sent to Charles Town by some of Brown's Northern supporters ostensibly to defend the raider chieftain; his real mission was to gather information that might be useful to those plotting Brown's escape.

As the trial progressed, Brown became more and more irritated with his court-appointed lawyers and openly expressed his lack of confidence in them. *Botts and Green thereupon withdrew, leaving Hoyt, the woefully inexperienced "beardless boy" who was entirely unacquainted with the code and procedure of the Virginia courts and knowing very little about the case, burdened with the sole responsibility for conducting the defense in one of the most sensational trials the country had ever witnessed. He was soon reinforced, however, by more seasoned counsel. Samuel Chilton of Washington, D.C., and Hiram Griswold of Cleveland, Ohio, were persuaded by Brown's influential friends to join the fight to save the abolitionist's life. But their arrival made little difference; the outcome of the trial was inevitable.*

The prosecution's parade of witnesses recounted the story of the attack on Harpers Ferry, the arming of the slaves, and the deaths of Hayward Shepherd, Fontaine Beckham, and George W. Turner. Brown's contention that, as commander in chief of a provisional army, he should be tried according to the laws of war and not as a common criminal was rejected. Other arguments offered by the defense met with equally fruitless results. Finally, on October 31, closing arguments by the prosecution and the defense were heard and at 1:45 p.m. the case went to the jury. Deliberations lasted for 45 minutes. The verdict: guilty on all three counts. A newspaper correspondent described the reaction:

Not the slightest sound was heard in the vast crowd as this verdict was thus returned and read. Not the slightest expression of elation or triumph was uttered from the hundreds present, who, a moment before, outside the court, joined in heaping threats and imprecations upon his head; nor was this strange silence interrupted during the whole of the time occupied by the forms of the Court. Old Brown himself said not even a word, but, as on previous days, turned to adjust his pallet, and then composedly stretched himself upon it.

Andrew Hunter, special prosecutor for the State of Virginia, vowed to see Brown "arraigned, tried, found guilty, sentenced and hung, all within ten days."

The courtroom in which Brown was tried was not as large as this drawing would indicate, but it was packed with witnesses and spectators. Brown lay on a cot during most of the proceedings, rising only occasionally to make a point in his defense. The insets show Jefferson County Sheriff James Campbell (left) and the jailer, John Avis.

Sentence was passed on November 2: John Brown would hang on Friday, December 2, 1859. The other raiders—Coppoc, Stevens, Copeland, and Green—were tried subsequently, found guilty, and received like sentences. Of the seven raiders who escaped from Harpers Ferry, John Cook and Albert Hazlett were captured in Pennsylvania, brought to Charles Town for trial, convicted, and hanged.

In the days following Brown's sentencing, Virginia's Governor Wise was swamped with mail. Many letters pleaded for clemency, some contained outright threats, while others warned of fantastic plots to effect the abolitionist's escape. Martial law was declared in Charles Town. Militiamen were everywhere, and armed patrols kept a vigilant watch on all roads leading into town. The day of execution came, and not one of the schemes to free Brown materialized.

Henry A. Wise,
Governor of Virginia

PROCLAMATION!

IN pursuance of instructions from the Governor of Virginia, notice is hereby given to all whom it may concern,

That, as heretofore, particularly from now until af er Friday next the 2nd of December, STRANGERS found within the County of Jefferson, and Counties adjacent, having no known and proper business here, and ho cannot give a satisfactory account of themselves, will be at once arrested.

That on, and for a proper period before that day, stangers and especially parties, approaching under the pretext of being present at the execution of John Brown, whether by Railroad or otherwise, will be met by the Military and turned back or arrested without regard to the amount of force, that may be required to effect this, and during the said period and especially on the 2nd of December, the citizens of Jefferson and the surrounding country are *EMPHATICALLY* warned to remain at their homes armed and guard their own property.

On the afternoon before the execution, Brown's grief-stricken wife was allowed to visit him in his cell. They spent several hours talking. Toward evening they parted, and Mary Brown went to Harpers Ferry to await the delivery of her husband's body. It would be her agonizing duty to return Brown's remains to their North Elba home for burial.

A few minutes after 11 a.m. on December 2, 1859, John Brown walked down the steps of the Charles Town jail, climbed into the back of a horse-drawn wagon, and sat down on his own coffin. Flanked by files of soldiers, the wagon moved off toward a field a short distance from the town where a scaffold had been erected. No civilians were permitted near the execution site. The field was ringed by 1,500 soldiers, among them a company of Virginia Military Institute cadets commanded by a stern-

With soldiers lining the streets, John Brown comes down the steps of the Charles Town jail on the way to his execution, December 2, 1859. The wagon containing his coffin stands nearby.

looking professor who would soon gain fame and immortality as the Confederate Gen. "Stonewall" Jackson. In the ranks of a Richmond company stood another man who, in a few short years, would also achieve immortality by committing one of the most infamous deeds in American history—John Wilkes Booth.

As the hushed military watched, Brown climbed the scaffold steps. Sheriff John W. Campbell pulled a white linen hood over the prisoner's head and set the noose. John Avis, the jailor, asked Brown to step forward onto the trap. "You must lead me," Brown replied, "for I cannot see." The abolitionist's last words were directed to Avis as one final adjustment of the noose was made. "Be quick," he said.

At 11:30 a hatchet stroke sprung the trap and John Brown died. The voice of a militia colonel broke the stillness: "So perish all such enemies of Virginia! All such enemies of the Union! All such enemies of the human race!"

But the end was not yet. True, Brown was dead; but he had helped to arouse popular passions both North and South to the point where compromise would be impossible. The raid created a national furor and generated a wave of emotionalism that widened the sectional breach that had divided the country for so many years. Although conservative Northern opinion quickly condemned the raid as the work of a madman, the more radical hailed it as "the best news America ever had" and glorified Brown as "the new saint" whose martyrdom in the cause of human freedom would make the gallows "glorious like the cross."

The hanging of John Brown took place at 11:30 a.m., December 2, 1859, in a field just outside Charles Town. The field no longer exists, but the site is identified by a simple stone marker.

Southerners shuddered. For decades they had been defending their "peculiar institution" of slavery against the ever-increasing attacks of Northern abolitionists, but anti-slavery agitation had always followed a course of non-violence. Then Brown had come with his pikes and guns to change all that. In the false atmosphere of crisis that gripped the South in the wake of the raid, the small voices of moderates were lost in the din of extremists who saw Brown's act as part of a vast Northern conspiracy to instigate servile insurrections throughout the slave States.

To meet this threat, real or imagined, vigilance committees were formed, volunteer military companies were organized, and more and more Southerners began to echo the sentiments of the Richmond Enquirer: "if under the form of a Confederacy our peace is disturbed, our State invaded, its peaceful citizens cruelly murdered . . . by those who should be our warmest friends . . . and the people of the North sustain the outrage, then let disunion come."

Disunion sentiment increased during the presidential campaign of 1860, stimulated by a split in the Democratic Party that practically guaranteed a Republican victory in the November elections. When Abraham Lincoln was elected President, the secessionist movement could no longer be contained. On December 20, unable to tolerate a President "whose opinions and purposes are hostile to slavery," South Carolina severed her ties with the Union. By February 1, 1861, Mississippi, Florida, Alabama, Georgia, Louisiana, and Texas had followed her lead. One week later the Confederate States of America was formed at Montgomery, Ala., and the country drifted slowly toward civil war. Before many months had passed, soldiers in blue would be marching south to the tune of "John Brown's Body" as if to fulfill the prophecy Brown had left in a note to one of his Charles Town guards shortly before the execution:

Charlestown, Va., 2ʳ December, 1859

I John Brown am now quite certain that the crimes of this guilty, land: will never be purged away; but with Blood. I had as I now think: vainly flattered myself that without very much bloodshed; it might be done.

EPILOGUE

The war that John Brown predicted would come, and which his raid helped to precipitate, began in April 1861. When it ended almost 4 years to the day later, slavery had been destroyed along with some 600,000 lives and millions of dollars worth of property. Among the casualties of the war was Harpers Ferry. The town's strategic position on the Baltimore and Ohio Railroad at the northern end of the Shenandoah Valley made it a prime target for both Union and Confederate forces. It changed hands again and again, and by war's end in 1865 the place was a shambles.

As early as February 1862 a young Union staff officer assigned to the Harpers Ferry area could write of the town: "The appearance of ruin by war and fire was awful. Charred ruins were all that remain of the splendid public works, arsenals, workshops and railroads, stores, hotels, and dwelling houses all mingled in one common destruction." Much the same observation was made 3 years later in the summer of 1865 by John T. Trowbridge, a New England writer, during a tour of the South: "[T]he town is the reverse of agreeable. It is said to have been a pleasant and picturesque place formerly. The streets were well graded, and the hill-sides above were graced with terraces and trees. But war has changed all. Freshets tear down the centre of the streets, and the hill-sides present only ragged growths of weeds. The town itself lies half in ruins. . . . Of the bridge across the Shenandoah only the ruined piers are left; still less remains of the old bridge over the Potomac. And all about the town are rubbish, filth and stench."

The once-imposing armory complex along the Potomac River and the rifle works on Hall Island in the Shenandoah were burned-out hulks. Only the armory enginehouse remained basically intact, "like a monument which no Rebel hands were permitted to demolish." Large sections of the town had been burned by various troop contingents to prevent their use by enemy soldiers. Many homes, churches, schools, and business establishments were damaged beyond repair by shot and shell fired from the surrounding heights. Still other buildings, subjected to long military use, were on the verge of ruin. The industries on Virginius Island—the iron foundry, the flour mill, the sawmill, the machine shops, the cotton mill—were also gone, and Harpers Ferry no longer had the activity and bustle of an economically healthy community.

Besides the material damage inflicted by powerful weaponry and by the seemingly endless procession of soldiers who filched or requisitioned everything that could be carried away, the town suffered an even greater loss—its people. During the war most of the townspeople moved away, some to escape the dangers of military operations, some to seek employment elsewhere after the armory and the industries were destroyed, and some to join one or the other opposing armies. Many never came back. Those who did return found their town in ruins and themselves the citizens of a new State.

In 1861 the people in the mountainous western counties of Virginia strongly opposed secession. When the rest of the State voted overwhelmingly in a statewide referendum on May 23, 1861, to withdraw from the Federal Union, the loyal western residents, in a series of conventions at Wheeling, voted to "secede" from Virginia and set up their own State. The bill for admission passed Congress on December 11, 1862, and on June 30, 1863, by Presidential proclamation, West Virginia became the 35th State. For years, however, many Jefferson County residents refused to use "West" as part of the designation.

Harpers Ferry never recovered from the devastation of the Civil War. Staring at the stark chimneys and charred remains of once impressive buildings, one of the townspeople concluded: "This place will never be anything again unless the government rebuilds the armory—and it is doubtful if that is ever done." The Government never did, and the ground on which it stood was auctioned off in 1869. Mills and factories remained closed. The railroad did a small percentage of its previous business. Hopes for a renewal of the town's former prosperity were dashed in 1870 when a flood destroyed or badly damaged nearly every building on Virginius Island and along the south side of Shenandoah Street. Subsequent floods destroyed still more of the town and ruined the Chesapeake and Ohio Canal. The canal was finally abandoned after the flood of 1924.

Inundated too often by high water, the residents of Harpers Ferry eventually left the old buildings in the lower town and moved up the heights to the high ground of Camp Hill and toward Bolivar. For years the old shops and stores, those that remained, stood empty, neglected, and deteriorating. When Harpers Ferry became a national historical area, the National Park Service began an intensive campaign to preserve the fragile remains of the 18th- and 19th-century industries, homes, churches, stores, and shops, and to restore much of the old town to its pre-Civil War appearance, a time when it was at its peak as a thriving, bustling industrial community and transportation center.

Today, while much of the old historical town remains, few of the structures that figured prominently in John Brown's raid survive. (See maps on pp. 29 and 30.) The Baltimore and Ohio Railroad bridge across the Potomac, by which Brown and his raiders entered Harpers Ferry in October 1859, was destroyed by Confederate soldiers early in the Civil War. More modern structures span the river now, but the stone supports of the old bridge can still be seen. Nothing at all remains of the bridge across the Shenandoah. The stone piers now standing in the river near the Point section of the town are from a later structure.

The ruins of the armory buildings stood for many years after the war and eventually disappeared. In 1893 the site itself disappeared under 30 feet of fill when the B & O Railroad changed the line of its tracks. The outlines of two of the armory buildings have been marked by flat stones and the spot where the enginehouse was located is marked by a small monument. The enginehouse itself (now called "John Brown's Fort") stands nearby on the old arsenal grounds, and is little changed from its appearance at the time of the raid. Here also can be seen the excavated remains of the small U.S. arsenal and some of the partially exposed burned muskets destroyed when the building was gutted by Federal troops in April 1861.

In February 1862 Federal soldiers burned the Point area of Harpers Ferry to keep Confederate sharpshooters from using the buildings. Among the structures destroyed were the railroad depot, the water tower around which Mayor Fontaine Beckham was peering when he was shot by one of the raiders, several stores and shops, the Potomac Restaurant, the Wager House Hotel, and the Gault House Saloon. The Wager House (not to be confused with another structure of the same name that still exists) was the scene of several notable events. It was here that many of the wounded were carried, including two of the raiders, Aaron Stevens and William Thompson. Many of the militiamen did their "best fighting" at its bar. From the Wager House porch, Gov. Henry Wise of Virginia read letters taken from Brown's men to the angered townspeople. Wise also lived here during his brief stay in Harpers Ferry. Mrs. John Brown stayed here when she came to Harpers Ferry in December 1859 for her last visit with her husband, and it was here that she received his body after the execution.

The Shenandoah islands are deserted today except for the line of the Winchester and Potomac Railroad. All of the buildings are gone now except for the foundations of some of the mills and the retaining walls of the rifle factory, nestled in among the weeds, brush, and trees. Many disappeared through neglect after the industries were destroyed during the Civil War, some washed away in the many floods with which Harpers Ferry has been plagued, and others, like Herr's flour mill and the rifle works, were deliberately destroyed by Union and Confederate troops.

Several structures associated with the raid still exist outside Harpers Ferry. The courthouse at Charles Town, W. Va., is little changed since John Brown was tried and sentenced there more than a century ago. The Kennedy farm, Brown's headquarters during the months he was planning the raid, lies in the Maryland countryside about 5 miles from Harpers Ferry. Col. Lewis Washington's home, "Beallair," which several raiders broke into on the night of October 16 and took its owner hostage, stands near Halltown, about 4 miles west of Harpers Ferry. And nearby, at the foot of Alstadt Hill, west of Bolivar, is the home of John H. Alstadt, another hostage taken by Brown's men on October 16.

APPENDIX

The Capture of John Brown*
by Israel Green

At noon of Monday, October 18, 1859, Chief Clerk Walsh, of the Navy Department, drove rapidly into the Washington Navy-yard, and, meeting me, asked me how many marines we had stationed at the barracks available for immediate duty. I happened to be the senior officer present and in command that day. I instantly replied to Mr. Walsh that we had ninety men available, and then asked him what was the trouble. He told me that Ossawatomie Brown, of Kansas, with a number of men, had taken the arsenal at Harper's Ferry, and was then besieged there by the Virginia State troops. Mr. Walsh returned speedily to the Navy Department building, and, in the course of an hour, orders came to me from Secretary Tousey to proceed at once to Harper's Ferry and report to the senior officer; and, if there should be no such officer at the Ferry, to take charge and protect the government property. With a detachment of ninety marines, I started for Harper's Ferry that afternoon on the 3:30 train, taking with me two howitzers. It was a beautiful, clear autumn day, and the men, exhilarated by the excitement of the occasion, which came after a long, dull season of confinement in the barracks, enjoyed the trip exceedingly.

At Frederick Junction I received a dispatch from Colonel Robert E. Lee, who turned out to be the army officer to whom I was to report. He directed me to proceed to Sandy Hook, a small place about a mile this side of the Ferry, and there await his arrival. At ten o'clock in the evening he came up on a special train from Washington. His first order was to form the marines out of the car, and march from the bridge to Harper's Ferry. This we did, entering the enclosure of the arsenal grounds through a back gate. At eleven o'clock Colonel Lee ordered the volunteers to march out of the grounds, and gave the control inside to the marines, with instructions to see that none of the insurgents escaped during the night. There had been hard fighting all the preceding day, and Brown and his men kept quiet during the night. At half-past six in the morning Colonel Lee gave me orders to select a detail of twelve men for a storming party, and place them near the engine-house in which Brown and his men had intrenched themselves. I selected twelve of my best men, and a second twelve to be employed as a reserve. The engine-house was a strong stone [actually brick] building, which is still in a good state of preservation at the Ferry, in spite of the three days' fighting in the building by Brown and his men, and the ravages of the recent war between the States. The building was . . . perhaps thirty feet by thirty-five. In the front were two large double doors, between which was a stone abutment. Within were two old-fashioned, heavy fire-engines, with a hose-cart and reel standing between them, and just back of the abutment between the doors. They were double-battened doors, very strongly made, with heavy wrought-iron nails.

---

*Originally published in *The North American Review*, December 1885.

Lieutenant J. E. B. Stewart [Stuart], afterwards famous as a cavalry commander on the side of the South, accompanied Colonel Lee as a volunteer aid. He was ordered to go with a part of the troops to the front of the engine-house and demand the surrender of the insurgent party. Colonel Lee directed him to offer protection to Brown and his men, but to receive no counter-proposition from Brown in regard to the surrender. On the way to the engine-house, Stewart and myself agreed upon a signal for attack in the event that Brown should refuse to surrender. It was simply that Lieutenant Stewart would wave his hat, which was then, I believe, one very similar to the famous chapeau which he wore throughout the war. I had my storming party ranged alongside of the engine-house, and a number of men were provided with sledge-hammers with which to batter in the doors. I stood in front of the abutment between the doors. Stewart hailed Brown and called for his surrender, but Brown at once began to make a proposition that he and his men should be allowed to come out of the engine-house and be given the length of the bridge start, so that they might escape. Suddenly Lieutenant Stewart waved his hat, and I gave the order to my men to batter in the door. Those inside fired rapidly at the point where the blows were given upon the door. Very little impression was made with the hammers, as the doors were tied on the inside with ropes and braced by the hand-brakes of the fire-engines, and in a few minutes I gave the order to desist. Just then my eye caught sight of a ladder, lying a few feet from the engine-house, in the yard, and I ordered my men to catch it up and use it as a battering-ram. The reserve of twelve men I employed as a supporting column for the assaulting party. The men took hold bravely and made a tremendous assault upon the door. The second blow broke it in. This entrance was a ragged hole low down in the right-hand door, the door being splintered and cracked some distance upward. I instantly stepped from my position in front of the stone abutment, and entered the opening made by the ladder. At the time I did not stop to think of it, but upon reflection I should say that Brown had just emptied his carbine at the point broken by the ladder, and so I passed in safely. Getting to my feet, I ran to the right of the engine which stood behind the door, passed quickly to the rear of the house, and came up between the two engines. The first person I saw was Colonel Lewis Washington, who was standing near the hose-cart, at the front of the engine-house. On one knee, a few feet to the left, knelt a man with a carbine in his hand, just pulling the lever to reload.

"Hello, Green," said Colonel Washington, and he reached out his hand to me. I grasped it with my left hand, having my saber uplifted in my right, and he said, pointing to the kneeling figure, "This is Ossawatomie."

As he said this, Brown turned his head to see who it was to whom
Colonel Washington was speaking. Quicker than thought I brought my
saber down with all my strength upon his head. He was moving as
the blow fell, and I suppose I did not strike him where I intended, for he
received a deep saber cut in the back of the neck. He fell senseless on
his side, then rolled over on his back. He had in his hand a short Sharpe's-
cavalry carbine. I think he had just fired as I reached Colonel
Washington, for the marine who followed me into the aperture made by
the ladder received a bullet in the abdomen, from which he died in a
few minutes. The shot might have been fired by some one else in the
insurgent party, but I think it was from Brown. Instinctively as Brown fell
I gave him a saber thrust in the left breast. The sword I carried was a
light uniform weapon, and, either not having a point or striking something
hard in Brown's accouterments, did not penetrate. The blade bent double.

By that time three or four of my men were inside. They came
rushing in like tigers, as a storming assault is not a play-day sport. They
bayoneted one man skulking under the engine, and pinned another
fellow up against the rear wall, both being instantly killed. I ordered the
men to spill no more blood. The other insurgents were at once taken
under arrest, and the contest ended. The whole fight had not lasted over
three minutes. My only thought was to capture, or, if necessary, kill,
the insurgents, and take possession of the engine-house.

I saw very little of the situation within until the fight was over. Then
I observed that the engine-house was thick with smoke, and it was
with difficulty that a person could be seen across the room. In the rear,
behind the left-hand engine, were huddled the prisoners whom Brown
had captured and held as hostages for the safety of himself and his
men. Colonel Washington was one of these. All during the fight, as I
understood afterward, he kept to the front of the engine-house. When I
met him he was as cool as he would have been on his own veranda
entertaining guests. He was naturally a very brave man. I remember that
he would not come out of the engine-house, begrimed and soiled as
he was from his long imprisonment, until he had put a pair of kid gloves
upon his hands. The other prisoners were the sorriest lot of people I
ever saw. They had been without food for over sixty hours, in constant
dread of being shot, and were huddled up in the corner where lay the
body of Brown's son and one or two others of the insurgents who had been
killed. Some of them have endeavored to give an account of the storming
of the engine-house and the capture of Brown, but none of the reports
have been free from a great many misstatements, and I suppose that
Colonel Washington and myself were the only persons really able to say
what was done. Other stories have been printed by people on the outside,
describing the fight within. What they say must be taken with a great
deal of allowance, for they could not have been witnesses of what
occurred within the engine-house. One recent account describes me as
jumping over the right-hand engine more like a wild beast than a
soldier. Of course nothing of the kind happened. The report made by

Colonel Lee at the time, which is now on file in the War department, gives a more succinct and detailed account than any I have seen.

I can see Colonel Lee now, as he stood on a slight elevation about forty feet from the engine-house, during the assault. He was in civilian dress, and looked then very little as he did during the war. He wore no beard, except a dark mustache, and his hair was slightly gray. He had no arms upon his person, and treated the affair as one of no very great consequence, which would be speedily settled by the marines. A part of the scene, giving color and life to the picture, was the bright blue uniform of the marines. They wore blue trousers then, as they do now, and a dark-blue frock-coat. Their belts were white, and they wore French fatigue caps. I do not remember the names of the twelve men in the storming party, nor can I tell what became of them in later life. We had no use for the howitzers, and, in fact, they were not taken from the car.

Immediately after the fight, Brown was carried out of the engine-house, and recovered consciousness while lying on the ground in front. A detail of men carried him up to the paymaster's office, where he was attended to and his wants supplied. On the following day, Wednesday, with an escort, I removed him to Charleston [Charles Town], and turned him over to the civil authorities. No handcuffs were placed upon him, and he supported himself with a self-reliance and independence which were characteristic of the man. He had recovered a great deal from the effects of the blow from my saber, the injury of which was principally the shock, as he only received a flesh wound. I had little conversation with him, and spent very little time with him.

I have often been asked to describe Brown's appearance at the instant he lifted his head to see who was talking with Colonel Washington. It would be impossible for me to do so. The whole scene passed so rapidly that it hardly made a distinct impression upon my mind. I can only recall the fleeting picture of an old man kneeling with a carbine in his hand, with a long gray beard falling away from his face, looking quickly and keenly toward the danger that he was aware had come upon him. He was not a large man, being perhaps five feet ten inches when he straightened up in full. His dress, even, I do not remember distinctly. I should say that he had his trousers tucked in his boots, and that he wore clothes of gray—probably no more than trousers and shirt. I think he had no hat upon his head.

None of the prisoners were hurt. They were badly frightened and somewhat starved. I received no wounds except a slight scratch on one hand as I was getting through the hole in the door. Colonel Lee and the people on the outside thought I was wounded. Brown had, at the time, only five or six fighting men, and I think he himself was the only one who showed fight after I entered the engine-house. There were no provisions in the building, and it would have been only a question of time when Brown would have had to surrender. Colonel Washington was the only person inside the house that I knew.

I have been asked what became of Brown's carbine. That I do not know. My sword was left in Washington, among people with whom I lived, and I lost trace of it. A few years ago, after having come out of the war and gone west to Dakota, where I now live, I received a letter from a gentleman in Washington, saying that he knew where the sword was, and that it was still bent double, as it was left by the thrust upon Brown's breast. He said that it was now a relic of great historic value, and asked me to assent to the selling of it upon the condition that I should receive a portion of the price of the weapon. To me the matter had very little interest, and I replied indifferently. Since then I have heard nothing of the matter. I presume the saber could be found somewhere in Washington.

 SELECTED READING LIST

Joseph Barry, The Strange Story of Harper's Ferry With Legends of The Surrounding Country, *Martinsburg, W. Va., 1903.*

Richard O. Boyer, The Legend of John Brown: A Biography and A History, *New York, 1973.*

Louis Filler, The Crusade Against Slavery, 1830-1860, *New York, 1960.*

Stephen B. Oates, To Purge This Land With Blood: A Biography of John Brown, *New York, 1970.*

Louis Ruchames, ed., John Brown: The Making of a Revolutionary, *New York, 1969. (Originally published under the title* A John Brown Reader.*)*

Franklin B. Sanborn, Life and Letters of John Brown, *Boston, 1885.*

Kenneth M. Stampp, The Peculiar Institution: Slavery in the Ante-Bellum South, *New York, 1956.*

Edward Stone, ed., Incident at Harper's Ferry, *Englewood Cliffs, 1956.*

Oswald Garrison Villard, John Brown, 1800-1859: A Biography Fifty Years After, *Boston and New York, 1911 (2d edition, 1943).*

☆U.S. Government Printing Office: 1973 0-521-267
Reprint 1990